Five Buckets of Leadership: SPEAKING IN THE MOMENT

by

DR. ANISSA REILLY

Little Rock

2021

Five Buckets of Leadership: Speaking in the Moment

Print ISBN 13: 978-1-949934-54-0

Copyright © 2021 by Dr. Anissa Reilly

Published by Faith 2 Fe Publishing,
PO Box 242692, Little Rock, AR 72223
www.publishyourfaith.com

Printed in the United States of America. All rights reserved under International Copyright Law. No part of this publication may be reproduced, stored in a retrieval system, or transmitted in any form or by any means-electronic, mechanical, photocopy, recording or any other-except for brief quotations in printed reviews, without the prior written permission of the author.

Foreword

If you are in a position where you have to speak in front of a large audience, answer questions, or represent your organization in events and you have ever struggled with articulating your thoughts in a concise manner, this manual is a must-read. It provides a concise process of organizing your thoughts into "buckets" for easy retrieval. It helps you to quickly, consistently, and confidently articulate the core mission and vision of your organization, thereby making it applicable in addressing day-to-day challenges and situations that you confront and are asked about. The principles can be applied in various industries and is an excellent training tool for new leaders and a great resource for seasoned ones.

Lanre Somorin MD
Author of *Seize Your Moment: Unmasking Everyday Opportunities*
CEO of ExodusHealth Medical PC.

CONTENTS

1. Who Should Read This Manual?...............................1
2. How to Use This Manual 3
3. Development of the Process...5
4. Phase 1: The "Main" Bucket— Write a Vision............13
5. Phase 2: Identify Bucket Carriers...... 19
6. Phase 3: Bucket Identification.....................................25
7. Phase 4: Bucket Belief 31
8. Phase 5: Bucket Response 43
9. Troubleshooting the Process.......................................65

Who Should Read This Manual?

As a leader, have you ever found yourself in a position struggling to answer a question? You may start off well and provide clear, concise thoughts. You may have even garnered the attention of the one who posed the question for a brief moment, and then, somewhere along the way, your response becomes lost and seemingly disconnected. Your palms start to sweat, your heart starts to race, and your mouth goes dry. You attempt to gather your thoughts and try to remember the question and point you were making, but it is too late. So, you end it with a polite smile as the one who was listening smiles back. Awkward!

Have you ever walked away from that encounter, wondering if you made any sense? Maybe your experience has not been as intimate as the one previously described. Perhaps your profession requires you to frequently speak before large audiences and respond to their questions afterward. You realize as you stand in front of these crowds, you are not only representing yourself but your organization. Who doesn't want to make a good impression? How can one do that without knowing what types of questions will be asked? If you have had these experiences, you are not alone, and this guidebook is for you. This guide will give some practical tools to use, and you will see immediate results in your confidence and ability to answer any question that is posed.

There is no magic bullet to answering questions or anticipating what will be asked; however, based on your field, you can predict the type of inquiries that will be made, and as a result, you can be prepared with a clear, concise solid response. This ability is grounded in a technique I have called the *"Five Buckets of Leadership: Speaking in the Moment."* I'll explain it more in the following chapter. This technique helps you to zero in on the heart of the question and respond accordingly. Often, we get bogged down with the details of the question and lose sight of the core inquiry. As an educator, I have used this whenever I speak to my staff, my community members, or other valuable stakeholders. Because of its design, any leader in any organization can apply the principles.

As I sat to express how I would share this technique, I vacillated between writing a book or a manual because I wanted you to feel as if we were having a conversation, as if I was standing right beside you, coaching you through the process. Therefore, I settled on a manual with the feel of a book. The manual will give you an opportunity to stop and practice some of the techniques we discuss. It will also allow you to easily go to a particular section for review.

How to Use This Manual

	ICON KEY
📁	Valuable Information
✏️	Test Your Knowledge
🗣️	Speaking Exercise
📖	Workbook Review

Before we begin, let me share with you how to use this manual. The "icon key" is your friendly manual navigator. Each icon serves a different purpose, and if you would like to get the most out of this manual, I highly suggest you give the icons some attention.

About the "Valuable Information" Icons

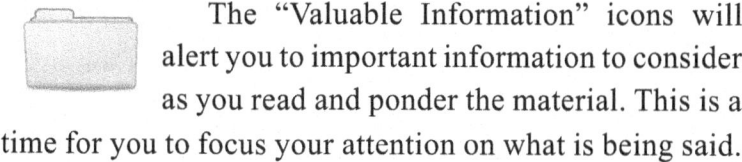

The "Valuable Information" icons will alert you to important information to consider as you read and ponder the material. This is a time for you to focus your attention on what is being said.

About the "Test Your Knowledge" Icons

The "Test Your Knowledge" icons will inform you that it is time to test your knowledge. Any new learning requires many opportunities for application to obtain mastery. This is your first opportunity.

About the "Speaking Exercise" Icons

The "Speaking Exercise" icons require you to stop and practice aloud the techniques just discussed. As a leader, when do you ever get to practice before it really counts? Some of us do, while others have never thought about its importance. This is a time to engage in a method that helps one get better.

About the "Workbook Review" Icons

The final icon, the "Workbook Review," provides you with an opportunity to write your thoughts, capture your ideas, take notes, and craft messages. It is crucial to write while your brain is creating new schema from the learning in which it is engaged.

As you go through the guide, I ask that you utilize the icons as suggested to get the full experience of this manual. As previously stated, it is written in a manner to feel as if I am right there with you coaching you through the process. The icons are my little helpers; therefore, use them.

Now that you know how to read this manual and how to use the little helpers along the way, it is time for you to have an open mind about a process that may seem simplistic at first. But I assure you, if done with fidelity and veracity, you will experience maximum results. *Five Buckets of Leadership: Speaking in the Moment* is Volume One in the series. This technique lends itself to other areas and is easily transferable to any arena.

Let's get started.

Development of the Process

The idea of the *Five Buckets of Leadership: Speaking in the Moment* came about when I became a principal. At the time, it was not a concept or technique. It was simply a way I found myself organizing my thoughts to address the myriad of decisions I had to make on a daily basis. When I say a *myriad*, I mean it felt as if each minute of the day a question needed to be answered, a problem needed an immediate resolution, or a solution needed to be instantly created. (One can argue, systems and structures were required to alleviate some of the pressure I seemed to face. I agree; however, that is for another volume in the series.)

With this barrage of inquiry coming fast and furious at one's brain, it could cause one to make critical mistakes, shut down, or withdraw if not properly equipped. I have always considered myself a fast-paced thinker and problem solver. But this pace would even weaken the most experienced. I knew that if I did not come up with a way to manage this, I would burn out quickly. To help, one of my mentors told me to slow down my internal processing, so I am clear about my decision making. This was a foreign request because I did not know how to "slow down." Thinking, in my opinion, is as natural as breathing. If you are not thinking, you are not living. For me, slowing down meant living at a slower pace. As the need to make decisions increased, I began to explore what my mentor asked.

Utilizing what I knew about the brain, I started there. Imagine the brain as a file cabinet. There is the main file cabinet, and if organized properly, each drawer contains information directly related to the main filing system. Labeling the cabinet drawers allows for easy retrieval and concise organization. Furthermore, labeling speeds up the process when one may find him or herself trying to locate a document. Have you ever experienced looking for paperwork, and because files were not labeled or labeled incorrectly, precious time was lost? Frustration, anxiety, and sometimes anger ensue. The flare-up of these emotions can compound the problem causing individuals to abandon the search. Like the filing cabinet, the brain has a built-in organizing system.

In their paper published in the journal *Neuron*[1], Lila Davachi, an NYU associate professor, and her co-author, Alexa Tompary describe in detail this system by outlining the role the hippocampus, a tiny portion of the brain, plays in consolidating and organizing information it receives

---

[1] Tompary A, Davachi L. Consolidation Promotes the Emergence of Representational Overlap in the Hippocampus and Medial Prefrontal Cortex. Neuron. 2017 Sep 27;96(1):228-241.e5. doi: 10.1016/j.neuron.2017.09.005. Erratum in: Neuron. 2020 Jan 8;105(1):199-200. PMID: 28957671; PMCID: PMC5630271.

through a process of identifying, extracting, and coding the most crucial parts of the experience for easy retrieval.

Gibbs, a specialist in leadership skills, explains it this way, "Whenever we need to make any decision in our personal or business life, our brain will go into what we have stored in its 'hard drive' to decide what to do."[2] Brain functioning has always been captivating to me, and its built-in filing system or "hard drive" added to my fascination. In my opinion, if we learned how to maximize the brain's functioning, especially the hippocampus, I believe it would transform a leader's ability to lead in their fast-paced environment.

Therefore, the first question I asked myself was, *"How do I approach any decision I make?"* Since I had never engaged in such a process, this was an interesting exploratory question. I began to pay close attention to my reaction time and how I answered questions. I also became attuned to the audience's reactions. Whether it was a single-member audience, a panel, or a crowd, their responses were clues that influenced my talk.

Once I was able to analyze my thought process, I categorized the method into five simple steps. To make the steps easily understood, I moved away from the scientific terminology of *hippocampus* and *prefrontal cortex* and imagined buckets. I am sure everyone has used a bucket or a bin of some sort; thus, I saw buckets as equipment that can be easily carried, filled, and emptied at a whim. Depending on how you use buckets, you can mimic the hippocampus by consolidating and organizing information for easy retrieval. Settling on this analogy

---
[2] Gibbs, Tomy. "7 Ways To Defeat Mental Muscle Memory." Tommy Gibbs, 24 June 2019, tommygibbstraining.com/7-ways-to-defeat-mental-muscle-memory/

was the beginning of how I began to capture my thought process in the moment. While becoming attuned to my thinking, I realized I went through a series of steps outlined below. These steps are the basis of this guide.

Phase 1- The "Main" Bucket

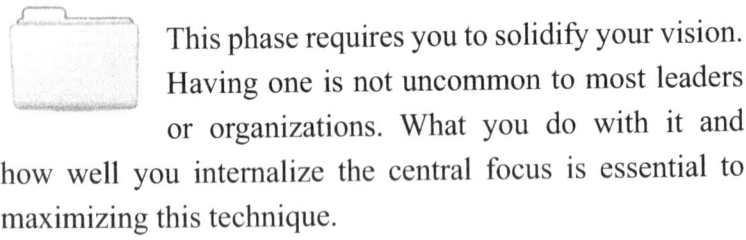

This phase requires you to solidify your vision. Having one is not uncommon to most leaders or organizations. What you do with it and how well you internalize the central focus is essential to maximizing this technique.

Phase 2- Bucket Carriers

Many people will call this step the mission. However true that may be, think for a moment a time where you have participated in the creation of a vision and a mission. For many, it was a long and arduous process. Oftentimes once the group was done, they emerged with a vision and mission that was verbose and hard to communicate, or the group simply wrote one because it had to be done. Sometimes the group would confuse the difference between the two. Whatever the scenario, most people would agree, it can be a complicated process. Therefore, it is my belief using the visual of a "bucket carrier" helps one to easily grasp the concept.

Phase 3 – Bucket Identification

Identifying the main topics of interest in your organization is the core activity for this step. Every organization has pillars that are central to its operations.

Once you can pinpoint the most crucial areas, the easier this step becomes.

Phase 4 – Bucket Belief

This step requires you to engage in some deep reflection around your core beliefs. You will need to zone in and isolate your personal standards and non-negotiables as they align with the previous steps. If you did not have a hand in creating your company's vision and mission, you will need to ensure the two are compatible. Any hint of misalignment will cause you to struggle with being authentic when speaking in the moment.

Phase 5 – Bucket Response

In my opinion, this phase is the most fun. It merges the previous four phases so that you are able to "speak in the moment." Here is where you get to practice, enabling you to respond clearly and concisely while sounding like a seasoned pro.

Separating my thinking this way was a good exercise, but was it just that? To answer this question, I began testing it out with various leadership mentees I was fortunately assigned to work alongside. During our conversations, I would share this process with hopes it would assist them in responding. To my delight, they reported it helped them in the most anxiety-driven situations. One mentee shared how the technique helped her during a 25-person panel interview for a leadership position. The panel consisted of teachers, parents, other school faculty, administrators, and school board members. She stated how her anxiety levels were up, and confidence was waning because of the large group. As they began firing questions at her, she described how the technique kicked in, and she could tell by their reactions that her responses were well received. Although she did not get the job, the superintendent personally called her and shared how impressed he was.

The more testimonies of success I heard, the more I shared the technique with colleagues and employees. It was becoming increasingly evident there was some truth to the technique. One of my mentees suggested I put it in a book to help others. I was reluctant at first. For me, it was not enough to have garnered success with those in my circle. I needed to know if there was any credibility to this, or was it simply a coincidence.

I began researching the science associated with the method, more specifically, the process outlined in Phase Five (Chapter Seven), to see if what I understood to occur in the brain held merit. To my surprise, the science validated what I knew and why success was being experienced at such a rapid rate. Before fully committing to writing about it, I continued to monitor what was occurring with those persons that fully engaged in the process. I continued to see positive results, so I decided to memorialize it.

Chapter Two Recap:

Your brain has the ability to organize information for easy retrieval. If we harness that ability, we can possibly increase our ability to lead in the moment. This can be done following a simple but effective thinking process. There are five phases to this technique. They were outlined in this chapter. What are they? In your own words, write a brief summary of each phase. See how many you can remember before looking back.

Phase 1: _____

Phase 2: _____

Phase 3: _____

Phase 4: _____

Phase 5: _____

Phase 1: The "Main" Bucket— Write a Vision

Analyzing your thought process is harder than you may think. It requires you to step out of yourself in real-time to become cognizant of how your brain is firing off rapid responses. After careful analysis, it became obvious that my decisions were anchored in my beliefs about the direction of the organization. Most people call it the vision. Wheatley and Kellner-Rogers (1996, p. 58) craft it as "…identity in motion."[3] Establishing a vision and being grounded in the beliefs it produces is central to how one makes decisions. If you are aware of where you are headed and how you want to get there, then you know what you can and cannot agree to.

Think for a moment about a time you went on vacation. For the purpose of this illustration, the destination is the

---

3 Wheatley, M. J., & Kellner-Rogers, M. (1996). Simpler Way. Berrett-Koehler.

Five Buckets of Leadership: Speaking in the Moment

 Galapagos Islands. When you arrive at the airport, there are many decisions required to get you to your destination. From which terminal are you departing? With what airline are you traveling? Are you checking baggage or only taking carry-on? What gate has been assigned for boarding? Perhaps you are departing from one of the larger airports that use shuttle service between gates. If so, what shuttle do you need? Do you have the right documents? The list goes on and on.

Amidst all of these decisions, you know the answers because you know where you are headed. Even if you find yourself at the wrong departure gate, you know how to course-correct because of your destination. *Side note: If you are like my husband, you do not like the hustle and bustle of traveling. He wishes we could snap our fingers and instantly find ourselves at our destination. If it were only that easy, we would have seen half of the world by now. Just like him, I too wish I could snap my fingers and find myself sitting on the actual beaches of the Galapagos Islands writing this manual. Instead, I am in my home office, listening to my neighbor mow his lawn. What a sound!* I have digressed.

My point is, knowing where you are headed (your vision) is central to your decision-making ability. Operating from your vision helps you to avoid last-minute decisions and unexpected events deterring you from your primary goal. In today's world, to describe vision, people are asking the question, *"What is your why?"* The question is posed in such a way to get at the core of why the listener does what he or she does every

Phase 1: The Main Bucket—Write a Vision

day. It is designed for the listener to hone in on his or her motivating factor. For example, the "Why?" behind one traveling to the Galapagos Islands could be because he or she likes to travel, or it is a need because it is therapeutic. In my opinion, the way vision is described or solicited is semantics. No discourse is needed. Whatever phrase you connect with, use that to fuel your ability to craft your vision. Fashioning a vision is what is central to this work.

When you are considering what your vision should be, remember that you were blessed with an imagination. Your imagination is the road on which your dreams travel. When you were little, you were asked, *"What do you want to be when you grow up?"* Without any knowledge about the profession, your imagination let your dream come forth, and you gave a response. Whether that was a fireman, policeman, dancer, lawyer, writer, etc., your imagination was the basis for your answer. This same principle applies when thinking about crafting a vision.

Now ask yourself, "Where do you see yourself, your organization?" Let your imagination take you there. Do not be afraid of the bigness or the seemingly impossible outcomes of where your imagination leads you. Simply embrace the journey and write down what you imagine.

_____

_____

_____

_____

For me, as the head of an elementary school, I envisioned my elementary school to be a safe haven for children where they would have access to authentic learning opportunities. I wanted them to be exposed to the rich culture of the arts while being equipped with the tools to be social activists. It included them being able to grapple with complex topics through the process of analyzing and synthesizing the information. People would say this was such a mighty vision for a school that served children from a low socio-economic status and whose state proficiency reading and math levels were below 5%. It would seem so in the present state, but I have never been one to accept the current state nor back down from a challenge. This was no different, especially since my imagination had taken me to this destination. Your imagination journey should not be any different.

Take a moment to reread what you wrote. Does it truly represent your imagination? Did you allow yourself to engage in the process fully? Did you hold back thinking it was not a possibility? If you answered no to any of these questions, I challenge you to imagine again and allow yourself to freely picture all of the possibilities. Imagine big! Write down all of the possibilities without restraint. Unless you share this, you are the only one who will read it, so there is minimal risk. Would it not be great when the vision comes to fruition, you can look back and read when it was simply a part of your imagination? I challenge you to take a leap of faith to imagine and record it in this book or in any other journal.

Phase 1: The Main Bucket—Write a Vision

Chapter Three Recap:

This chapter was about establishing a vision. A travel analogy was used to bring to life its importance. According to the chapter, why is a vision crucial for any organization?

_____
_____
_____
_____
_____
_____
_____
_____
_____
_____
_____
_____
_____
_____
_____
_____

Phase 2: Identify Bucket Carriers

After understanding where the school was headed, I had to answer the little questions that would help me get there, those little specific details that the vision would ride on. I will call them *bucket carriers*. Pointing back to the travel analogy to the Galapagos Islands, the "main" bucket or vision is traveling to the actual islands. The bucket carriers would be the specifics such as the departure gate, the airline, the documents, etc. Make sense? These little specifics help to make the vision a reality. They are constant, never changing, very predictable. To provide more clarity, when you travel, you will always need to know the departure gate, the airline, and need to have specific documents, etc. Without them, you will have trouble reaching your destination. Some people may call these specifics a mission, but we will call them the bucket carriers for the purpose of the *Five Buckets of Leadership: Speaking in the Moment*. I created three bucket carriers to help obtain the main bucket for my school. They were as follows: *intensive small-group instruction, a plethora of critical thinking opportunities (in written and oral formats), and student-led discussions.* These three bucket carriers were central to getting to our destination.

As stated in the previous chapter, my main bucket or vision for the school was creating a safe haven for children. It was important that students were engaged in a productive struggle with high-level authentic content and materials. This would be enriched by exposing them to a wide array of knowledge that included all art forms. To accomplish this goal, I had to decide the best way to carry the "main bucket." Here is my rationale for my bucket carriers.

Bucket Carrier Number 1: *Intensive small group instruction* allows students to formulate relationships in smaller numbers. It allows for students to collaborate with individuals in a risk-free environment. They have come to know and trust each other in their small groups, thereby creating the safe haven I imagined.

Bucket Carrier Number 2: *A plethora of critical thinking opportunities* teaches and exposes students to how to grapple with and analyze subject matter. It shows them how to look at information from a variety of angles before accepting the first idea displayed. Having students learn this way opens them up to ask questions and hopefully gives them a platform for respecting each other's thoughts and opinions.

Bucket Carrier Number 3: *Student led-discussions* are essential to the whole process because it is the application of the first two buckets. When students have

Phase 2: Identify Bucket Carriers

ownership of and feel empowered during their educational journey, they are more likely to be receptive to the nuances in the world around them. They are more likely to be creative and solution-oriented because leading a discussion means my voice matters.

The implementation of these three bucket carriers was crucial to obtaining the "main bucket." Without understanding what or how we were doing the work, we would have gotten lost along the way and ultimately lost our "Why," never manifesting the vision.

As you think about your bucket carriers, consider what it will take to reach your destination or your "Why." Decide on three to five carriers. They will change along the way as you get closer and closer to your destination. For instance, there are times when you encounter traffic on your way to the airport, so you find another route, or while you are at the departure gate, it changes. The destination has not changed. The means by which it will be obtained has. So, take a few moments to capture what you believe are your bucket carriers.

1. _____

_____

2. _____

_____

3. _____

_____

(What you believe are your bucket carriers...continued)

4. _____

_____

5. _____

_____

Now that you have identified the "main bucket" and your bucket carriers, you are going to need these as we move forward with the technique. If you have not taken the time to capture your vision and the carriers, the remainder of the manual will not be as effective. These two are essential ingredients for grounding your ability to master the technique I am about to explain. Thus, if you have recorded your thoughts, let's move on, and if you have not, I invite you to go back and jot down where your imagination takes you.

Chapter Four Recap:

Chapter Four discussed bucket carriers.
Answer the following two questions to test your understanding. Refer back to the text if clarity is needed.

What is another way to explain the phrase "bucket carrier"? _____

_____

_____

_____

Phase 2: Identify Bucket Carriers

Why are bucket carriers essential to this process?

_____

_____

_____

_____

_____

Phase 3: Bucket Identification

There are basic principles and structures in every organization. They range from the types of employees to the products and profits being the bottom line. It may be strange, at first, to apply these principles and structures to an educational organization; however, it applies. The product in schools, if you would allow, are the students to which we add value. Each institution of learning is required to add value to their students. At the end of every school year, children should leave their school further along than when they started in September. The better the product, in this case, the children, the more likely the public will want your services.

This same concept can be applied to profits. For schools, profits are likened to the amount of academic progress your students are making. Huge profits indicate a successful business model: thus, huge academic gains (profits) align with effective pedagogical practices. What does all of this mean? This is a way to demonstrate whatever organization you find yourself leading; the principles are the same. Master the principles, and you will be a more effective leader.

Every organization has pillars that are central to its functioning. There are areas companies frequently address because they are central to the daily operations. Knowing and attending to these areas affects the profit margin. Leaders can become more effective if these areas become second nature to their process of decision-making. Once leaders are able to pinpoint the most crucial areas, the easier this step becomes.

The Primary Principle, in regard to the *Five Buckets of Leadership: Speaking in the Moment* is identifying the five main topics surrounding your organization. Think about the many conversations you engage in about the organization you lead. When you narrow the talks and remove all of the fluff, what are you essentially discussing? In education, the top five are 1. Safety, 2. Parent Engagement, 3. Staff Development/support, 4. Curriculum, and 5. Student Data. Some may argue there are others, and I agree. But these are the top five and when you examine the others more closely, you will notice those other topics more than likely align with one of these five.

For instance, social-emotional learning (SEL) is a hot topic today. One or two things are normally discussed when this topic enters the conversation. The first, "What SEL curriculum do you use?" or second, "How do you support your students' SEL and growth?" The first is a bit more obvious to align because of the word *curriculum* in the question. The second is not as easy. When you analyze the core of this second question, you will realize

Phase 3: Bucket Identification

it is asking, "How are you ensuring and supporting your student's emotional and psychological safety?"; thus aligning with the topic of safety.

If you still do not agree, remember I asked you to have an open mind about this process so that it will not deter you from learning the technique. If you are an educator and believe there are another top five, then use those. My request of you is to master the concept more than disputing the top five. As a review, the primary principle is narrowing down the five main topics discussed in your field. I suggest you write down as many as you can and begin to group them into categories.

Once you have your categories, narrow them down to five. "Why five?" you ask. According to Cowan, your working memory is capable of holding approximately five "chunks" of high cognitive information (p.88).[4] The usage of the word *chunks* is taken from Miller's *Psychological Review* article that focuses on "the ability to increase effective storage capacity through the use of intelligent grouping or "chunking' of items" (as cited in Cowan, 2001).[5] It is this "chunking" concept that undergirds the *Five Buckets of Leadership: Speaking in the Moment.*

Remember, we are working with our brain, more specifically the hippocampus, to maximize its filing and retrieval process. Since science tells us the amount of information our working memory can comfortably manipulate, it is in our best interest to leverage that to

---

[4] Cowan, N. (2001). The magical number 4 in short-term memory: A reconsideration of mental storage capacity. Behavioral and brain sciences, 24(1), 87-114.
[5] Miller, A. L., Gross, M. P., & Unsworth, N. (2019). Individual differences in working memory capacity and long-term memory: The influence of intensity of attention to items at encoding as measured by pupil dilation. Journal of Memory and Language, 104, 25-42.

Five Buckets of Leadership: Speaking in the Moment

become better at navigating high pressured situations. Consequently, we work with the top five areas.

By now, you should have categorized your list into five categories, also known as chunks or buckets. List them here:

1. _____
2. _____
3. _____
4. _____
5. _____

Chapter Five Recap:

Chapter Five discussed how every organization has pillars that are central to their operations. Once you are able to pinpoint the most crucial areas, the easier this step becomes. Take a moment to jot down your thoughts to the following prompts:

What do you think about the primary principle?

_____
_____
_____
_____
_____
_____

Phase 3: Bucket Identification

How do you see yourself being more effective if you are clear about the five main areas in your business or organization?

_____

_____

_____

_____

_____

_____

Phase 4: Bucket Belief

What do we do with these five buckets? I am so glad you asked. Your five buckets will help you formulate a standard response for each category. In education, the five buckets we have identified for this exercise are 1. Safety, 2. Parent Engagement, 3. Staff Development/support, 4. Curriculum, and 5. Student Data. As you work through this part, find a nice quiet space free from distractions so you can think. You will need to engage in some deep reflection to get to the heart of the matter and discover what is truly important to you.

If you are employed by an organization, this will require you to find out what this means for you and your values to be separate and apart from your employer's. You will need to ensure the company's central standards are compatible with what is ultimately important to you. If not, you will struggle with being able to authentically speak in the moment. When this happens, you could potentially be perceived as disingenuous or untrustworthy. (Learning how to communicate when there is misalignment is for another manual in this series.)

For all of the entrepreneurs engaging in this reflective moment, you are free to do so without being concerned about the separation of values like your "corporate employed" counterparts. For those of you—corporate employed or entrepreneur—that are clear concerning their fundamental ideals, reassessing whether or not you are living them out is always productive. Let the alignment between your lived reality and your desires be the basis of your reflection.

To start, choose one of your buckets, and ask yourself, *"What is my core belief about this bucket?"* When thinking about your core belief, you want to narrow it down to one sentence. Operating this way makes effective use of your brain's storage capacity. Remember, your working memory can successfully navigate five chunks of information at a time. For example, my one-sentence core belief about the "safety bucket" is: "Safety is a non-negotiable that extends beyond physical safety to one's emotional and psychological well-being." My belief may seem basic, but it gives me room to maneuver, a technique I will unpack in Phase Five. Keeping it simple, in this case, keeping it to one sentence does not overwhelm the brain's storage capacity. This is essential to speaking in the moment.

Besides what we have learned about the amount of information the working memory can hold at one time, high-pressured moments heighten anxiety and stress levels, causing the brain to momentarily restructure how it transmits and receives information. Dr. Bruce McEwen, a neuroscientist from Rockefeller University, explains how stress-induced events cause the brain to restructure how it sends signals via the neurons involved in the working memory. This restructuring process is the brain's built-in safety measure that diverts functioning to addressing the task at hand.[6]

In her article, "How Stress Can Shrink your Brain and 6 Ways to Keep it from Happening," Stephanie Booth referenced a study published online in the journal *Neurology* that assessed the memory and thinking skills of their participants who were exposed to stressful situations.[7] Based on the brain images, it appeared the brain decreased in size, thus impacting the hippocampus' ability to function properly.[8]

Yes, the brain seemingly shrinks as a response to stress. Similarly, McEwen shares how prolonged exposure to stress has the potential to permanently refashion the operating system of the brain. He explains how stress-induced situations interrupt your brain's normal way of communicating over your neuron pathway.

This concept was brought to life during a hands-on training in which I participated. The activities involved recreating possible scenarios we as principals could possibly encounter so we could think about and practice what one could do if such a high-anxiety-producing event occurred while school was in session. During the training,

---

6 Epstein, R. H. (2020, February 10). Bruce McEwen, 81, is dead; Found stress can alter the brain. The New York Times. https://www.nytimes.com/2020/02/10/science/bruce-s-mcewen-dead.html
7 Booth, S., (2018, November, 21). How stress can shrink your brain and 6 ways to keep it from happening.Healthline. https://www.healthline.com/health-news/how-stress-can-shrink-your-brain#How-to-stay-ahead-of-your-stress
8 Echouffo-Tcheugui, J. B., Conner, S. C., Himali, J. J., Maillard, P., DeCarli, C. S., Beiser, A. S., ... & Seshadri, S. (2018). Circulating cortisol and cognitive and structural brain measures: The Framingham Heart Study. Neurology, 91(21), e1961-e1970.

a light-hearted, somewhat humorous story was shared, which I believe demonstrates how the brain functions in stressful situations. The story went as follows:

> *Under normal circumstances, we are all able to use our keys to open the doors to our homes. It is an act many can do without thinking. Now, consider that same scenario when you have to make it to the restroom in an emergency. You may start off swaying or begin a two-step jig as you attempt to open your door. You are turning the key, but the door is not opening. The more you try to turn the key; the urge to use the potty becomes stronger. You remove the key and begin to fiddle through them to find the right one. They drop, and now, it seems to make it in time will not happen. Your stress levels have now shot up because there is a possibility a major accident is about to occur right outside your home.*
>
> *It is at that moment your brain comes to the rescue and zeroes in on your keys. You focus on the exact key, and for a moment, the urge seems to leave. All concentration is geared towards opening the door, it does, and you make the dash to relieve yourself. You made it. Joy floods your mind and body while you begin your normal, after-work, wind down routine. Later that evening, you are looking for your keys, only to remember you left them in the door as you scrambled to get in.*

Perhaps this is not a relatable incident; however, I am quite sure you have encountered moments where all you could do was mentally attend to the immediate task. Whether that was turning down the music so you can concentrate while driving during a rainstorm or receiving news that you have just won the jackpot for your state's

Phase 4: Bucket Belief

lottery, your brain will readjust so you can assess a course of action amid the stress. (I just reengaged some of you with the last scenario.) These short bouts of stress may not have the profound effect noted in the previously mentioned study; however, science tells us, "Stress has the ability to physically shrink your brain."[9]

Since we have a basic idea of how the brain responds in these types of real-life scenarios, it would seem beneficial to lessen the amount of information it has to synthesize. Therefore, internalizing a basic statement—like the one I previously shared—about your beliefs will make it easier for your brain to retrieve it when you need to provide a succinct response in seemingly chaotic or high-stakes situations.

With that said, use the following table to write down your core beliefs for each of your "five buckets." As you write, see if you can craft a simple sentence with 20 words or less. Incorporate three to four high-leverage words that will help to trigger another thought. Mine are in bold in the chart. Creating a sentence with these parameters may take you through several revisions before you have a final product. Give yourself permission and the freedom to explore, bringing voice to your inner thoughts, beliefs, and core values in a non-traditional way. I am confident if you fully engage with this step, you will have a solid foundation for being able to speak in the moment with fidelity, sincerity, and intelligence.

---

[9] Booth, S., (2018, November, 21). How stress can shrink your brain and 6 ways to keep it from happening.Healthline. https://www.healthline.com/health-news/how-stress-can-shrink-your-brain#How-to-stay-ahead-of-your-stress

Bucket Identification	Core Belief
Example: Safety	*Example: It is a **non-negotiable** that extends beyond physical to one's emotional and psychological well-being.*

Phase 4: Bucket Belief

Reread what you wrote to make sure it is one sentence with high leverage words. Ask yourself, is it too wordy? Are there words you can eliminate to further narrow down your sentence to an even simpler form? Are your high-leverage words poignant enough to trigger a thought pattern that you can follow without a struggle? Remember, science teaches us high-pressured situations rewire our brain's neurotransmitters. A simple sentence with trigger words reduces the amount of data our brain has to navigate.

If you are having difficulty, or maybe you are not sure if the sentence can be revised again, consider recording yourself saying it. View it and listen to see what thoughts are triggered for you. Do those thoughts match your core beliefs? If the answer is yes, then the sentence should be complete. If not, repeat the process until it aligns. Be patient with yourself if the process has to be repeated several times.

Now that your sentences have been stripped down to their simplest form, I invite you to engage in a speaking exercise. Most electronic devices have audio and visual recording capabilities, so use that feature to visually record yourself saying your sentences about three or four times. (If you cannot use your device, stand in front of a mirror and complete the exercise.) Do your best to say it the same way each time so that there is some continuity in the recording. Imagine yourself already engaged in a conversation, and you happen to insert this sentence about your core beliefs. Be as natural as possible. Challenge yourself to push past the weird feeling you may be experiencing as you record. You will be glad you did.

Watch it and pay close attention to your facial expressions to see if there is alignment with what you are saying.

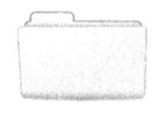

What is the importance of the alignment, you ask? Well, body language is an essential ingredient in communicating, especially when it is done extemporaneously. Sometimes, the nonverbal clues observed by others speak louder than what you are saying. According to Segal, Smith, Robinson, and Boose, "[Nonverbal cues] can put people at ease, build trust, and draw others towards you, or they can offend, confuse, and undermine what you're trying to convey" (para. 2).[10] The closer the alignment between the words you are saying and your body language, the more likely you are to connect with your audience and build a relationship of reliability.

As you analyze the recording to see what your face naturally does, be cognizant of what messages you may be unconsciously communicating and how they can be perceived. Did you raise your eyebrow on a certain word? Did you smirk at the end? How about your eyes? Were you able to maintain eye contact, or did you look away? If you notice any misalignment, think about why. Could it be the word choice? Did your eyes divert because you were thinking? Perhaps you are like me, and you are a naturally expressive person. Whatever is the underlying cause, awareness is key.

As you are analyzing yourself, write down what you notice, and the improvements

---

10 Segal, Ph.D., J., Smith, M.A., M., Robinson, L., & Boose, G. (2019, June) Non-verbal communication and body language. https://www.helpguide.org/articles/relationships-communication/nonverbal-communication.htm?pdf=13755

made as you practice. Jot down what you attribute to the changes.

_____

_____

_____

_____

_____

Knowing and understanding your non-verbal cues will aid in your ability to be genuine. If you realize the cause of the mismatch is your word choice, then choose another word. If the mismatch is part of who you are, then you can work on how expressive you may or may not need to be. Understand that totally controlling your natural body language is unrealistic. If you do try to control it, you could appear rather odd; thus, decreasing trust and rapport. However, employing the concept of the *Five Buckets of Leadership: Speaking in the Moment* can improve how you communicate nonverbally by developing **intellectual muscle memory**. (A term I created and will explain in Chapter Seven.)

Chapter Six Recap:

Chapter Six speaks about the science behind what happens to the functioning of the brain during stress-induced situations. In short, how the brain adapts and changes in these high-pressured instances. The chapter also dissected the role body language has in connecting with the audience. Take a moment to jot down thoughts to the following questions:

1. Think of a time when you were in a high-pressured situation and could not complete a seemingly easy task. Describe that moment and how it felt.

_____
_____
_____
_____
_____
_____

2. Referring to the moment you just described, what do you know now that could potentially create a different outcome?

_____
_____
_____
_____
_____
_____

3. Think of a time when someone was talking with you and his or her body language did not match the words that were proceeding out of that person's mouth. Describe that moment and how it felt. Was it difficult to stay focused?

Phase 4: Bucket Belief

How did you feel about the individual at the conclusion of the conversation?

_____
_____
_____
_____
_____
_____

4. Referring to the moment you just described, what do you know now that could have potentially created a different outcome?

_____
_____
_____
_____
_____
_____

Phase 5: Bucket Response

In Chapter One, we realized there is a way to answer questions succinctly when placed in anxiety-driven moments. Chapter Two taught us how our brain organizes and stores information and how that aligns with the *Five Buckets Speaking in the Moment*. The importance of having a vision in this process was discussed in Chapter Three by unpacking the idea of how important it is to know where you are going, or in some arenas, "your why" for doing something. Knowing your why gives greater meaning to what you are doing. Chapter Four furthered the heart of the previous chapter by explaining the need for bucket carriers.

As the implementation of the process started to narrow, Chapter Five explained the importance of identifying the pillars that are central to your company's daily operations and how they align with who you are and your fundamental ideology. Your first opportunity to practice occurred in Chapter Six. Not only did you become exposed to how the brain communicates during stressful situations, but you also learned about your core beliefs and what you may or may not be consciously or unconsciously communicating with your words and body language.

As promised, this chapter will outline the technique. As a reminder, I stated in Chapter One that the method might seem basic. But I will reiterate that you will experience maximum results if done with fidelity and veracity. This process I am about to share is all about retraining your brain about how to respond in stress-induced environments so that you can communicate effectively, succinctly, and as intelligently as possible.

This five-step process requires the most thought and practice. Practicing prior to needing the skill is vital to how much success you will experience and how well you will be able to implement it without much effort. It involves you being intentional and will take time to master. During this phase, you will learn how to use your "main" bucket, bucket carries, and core beliefs to answer the top five most asked content questions in your field. To assist, create a bank of questions by surveying hiring managers or other leaders in your particular profession. Once your list is compiled, categorize them to identify the trends noticed and how they align with the top five areas in your field. Since education is my expertise, the questions will be education-based for the purpose of this exercise.

When engaged in a stress-induced situation, such as a press conference, school board meetings, question and

Phase 5: Bucket Response

answer sessions, or an interview, once you are asked a question, the *Five Buckets of Leadership: Speaking in the Moment* technique is as follows:

1. Breathe deeply.
2. Identify the bucket with which the question aligns.
3. Retrieve your bucket belief to form the basis of your response.
4. Include specifics from your vision and vision carriers based on the nature of the question.
5. Smile and answer the question.

I told you the technique seemed rather simplistic. However, it is not so much about how simple the method appears, but how it functions within the psyche while the brain restructures how it transmits information during stressful events. Think about this technique as a way to trick the brain into thinking the stress has either lessened or has been removed. You can also think about it as a way to hijack the brain's transmittal process while it is compensating for the effects the stress is causing. Hence, the need to practice it until you become skilled is required.

As you practice, train yourself to run through each step in the exact order written. Do not miss a step. Each one is significant and builds upon the next. Each step works in concert with the other to interrupt how the brain is communicating at that moment. As you are practicing, you are building what I like to call intellectual muscle memory. *Merriam-Webster Dictionary* defines *muscle memory* as "the ability to repeat a specific muscular movement with improved efficiency and accuracy that is acquired through practice and repetition."[11] The goal, as noted in *Wikipedia*, is having the ability to complete the specific task "…with little to no conscious effort."[12]

Some activities that involve muscle memory are dancing, tying your shoes, riding a bicycle, driving, throwing a ball, or typing on a keyboard. With repeated proper practice, activities like these can be accomplished with little to no thought. It can be argued that muscle tissues do not have a "memory." While theoretically, this is true, the thinking behind the concept is what is key. A study posted in *Live Science,* an online magazine, noted that although muscle cells do not have the capacity to preserve a memory, "Your nerves have learned in which order to activate your muscles in order to perform a certain movement."[13] Stop here for a moment and think about an activity you routinely engage in that involves muscle memory. Perhaps it is tying a shoe or playing an instrument. Jot down what it feels like in your body and how much effort it takes.

To get a jumpstart, put down this manual and engage in one of the activities mentioned paying close attention to what you are experiencing internally.

---

11 "Muscle memory." Merriam-Webster.com Dictionary, Merriam-Webster, https://www.merriam-webster.com/dictionary/muscle%20memory. Accessed 28 Jan. 2021.
12 "Muscle Memory," Wikipedia, Wikimedia Foundation, 11-29-2020, https://en.wikipedia.org/wiki/Muscle_memory
13 Ghose, Tia. "'Muscle Memory' May Not Really Exist." LiveScience, Purch, 22 Sept. 2016, www.livescience.com/56218-muscles-have-no-strength-memory.html.

Phase 5: Bucket Response

Now think about an activity you learned that involved muscle memory but have not completed in a while. Perhaps you were a gymnast and could easily do a backflip, or maybe you were a figure skater. For many of us, this activity may be riding a bicycle. Think about a moment you attempted to accomplish this learned task after much time has passed. Jot down what it felt like to try again. Consider how much effort it took to do it again.

_____

_____

_____

_____

What you were able to capture in the two reflections is muscle memory at work in your body. Applying this concept to the term *intellectual muscle memory* involves the same basic principle. Since the brain has been referred to as a muscle (*It is an organ, not a muscle.*), more specifically a thinking muscle, it can be improved or strengthened through cognitive building brain exercises.

Many studies have discovered the positive effects such exercises have on the functioning of the brain's neurotransmitters.[14] I believe if properly trained or "exercised," the nerves that carry the neurotransmitters in your brain, like those in your muscles, can learn in which order to respond when quick thinking is required.

---

14 Santos-Longhurst, A., (2019, April 8). What is the physical composition of the human brain?. Healthline. https://www.healthline.com/health/is-the-brain-a-muscle#is-brain-activity-like-exercise

Consequently, the term intellectual muscle memory was birthed out of this connection. You may have heard of a similar term called mental muscle memory as described by Edward Mills.15 Unlike "mental muscle memory," where the learned thought patterns result in negative outcomes such as procrastination or low self-esteem, intellectual muscle memory is designed to create an alternative thinking map to be used when called upon amid intense moments. Like muscle memory, intellectual muscle memory is built over time with proper repeated practice.

Imagine what is happening in your mind as you go through this process. You are literally building a mind "roadmap" that will bypass your brain's normal way of functioning in a crisis so it can quickly access its filing system or "hard drive" in order to guide your neurotransmitters to give you the ability to speak concisely in the moment. Whew, that was a lot, but that is what is occurring in a nanosecond during this five-step process. As we delve into the science associated with each step, we know and understand steps one, two, and five happen in real time, while steps three and four, when practiced and internalized with fidelity, will happen automatically.

The Science Behind Each Step:

Step 1: *Breathe Deeply*

In the midst of tense situations, it is important to allow yourself to take a moment and breathe. Breathing has been shown to have positive effects on the

---

15 Mills, E., (n.d.). Mental muscle memory. International Mental Game Coaching Association. https://www.mentalgamecoaching.com/IMGCAArticles/Learning/MentalMuscleMemory.html

Phase 5: Bucket Response

body when you find yourself in these types of moments. The University of Michigan: Michigan Medicine reports the following:

> *Deep breathing is one of the best ways to lower stress in the body. This is because when you breathe deeply, it sends a message to your brain to calm down and relax. The brain then sends this message to your body. Those things that happen when you are stressed, such as increased heart rate, fast breathing, and high blood pressure, all decrease as you breathe deeply to relax.*[16]

As you can see, breathing is the first step to stopping the negative effects the stress is causing in your brain and body. You can breathe deeply on your own, or you can experience the maximum benefits by learning how to do it correctly. When you are breathing deeply in the proper way, you are engaging your upper and lower chest. In the beginning, it will take a conscious effort, and with continued practice, it will become muscle memory. Proper deep-breathing techniques can be found on the Michigan Medicine website found in the references of this book.

Besides, breathing provides an opportunity to think about the question asked so you can engage in the next three steps.

The next three steps work in tandem. They are: **Step Two:** *Identify the bucket with which the question aligns.* **Step Three:** *Retrieve your bucket belief to form the basis of your response.* **Step Four:** *Include specifics from your vision and vision carriers based on the nature of the question.*

---
[16] "Stress Management: Breathing Exercises for Relaxation." Stress Management: Breathing Exercises for Relaxation | Michigan Medicine, www.uofmhealth.org/health-library/uz2255.

49

Identifying the specific bucket that the question aligns with ensures you answer the question asked and eliminate extraneous information. Furthermore, it allows you the mental space needed to be succinct and brief. It focuses your thoughts in one direction to avoid distractors.

As cited on Course Hero (2015), an online study platform, Creswell terms this way of concentrating as "Focus on a single phenomenon concept."[17] He claims that focusing on one idea "… allows you to stay on task and gather more in detailed information. If you add focus on more than one phenomenon, then your research can become cloudy due to the amount of information you are trying to gather." Although this may appear specific to research, it aptly describes the importance of identifying one concept on which to focus. Another way of thinking about this is a "concept map."

According to The Learning Center at the University of North Carolina at Chapel Hill, concept maps are:

> "…visual representations of information…. They are a powerful study strategy because they help you see the big picture—because they start with higher-level concepts, they help you chunk information based on meaningful connections. In other words, knowing the big picture makes details more significant and easier to remember. Concept maps work very well…in times when it is important to see and understand relationships between different things. They can also be

---

17 Course Hero (2015). Focus on a single phenomenon or concept focusing on. Ashford University. Retrieved August 26, 2020, https://www.coursehero.com/file/p26i-bag6/Focus-on-a-single-phenomenon-or-concept-Focusing-on-one-concept-allows-you-to/

used to analyze information and compare and contrast." [18]

Let's highlight two pieces of information in this description to help actualize this step. The first, "...[concept maps] help you chunk information based on meaningful connections.

As previously discussed in Chapter Five, the brain can successfully manipulate five pieces of information at a time. Hence, having your thoughts create a concept map as a way to help process information by separating the specific details from the original big picture to create another big picture works in conjunction with how the brain processes information.

Perhaps this image will produce more clarity:

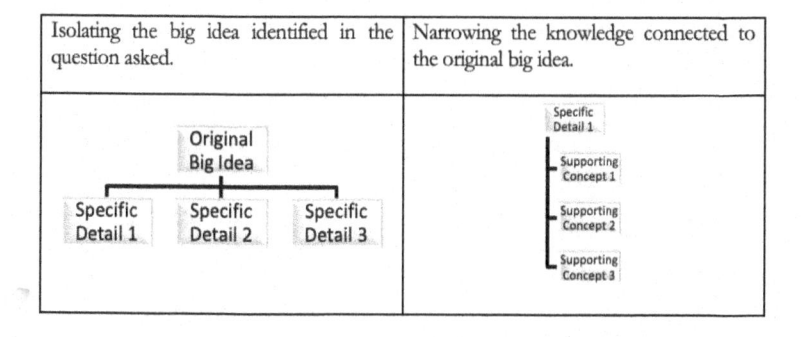

Isolating the big idea identified in the question asked.	Narrowing the knowledge connected to the original big idea.
Original Big Idea — Specific Detail 1, Specific Detail 2, Specific Detail 3	Specific Detail 1 — Supporting Concept 1, Supporting Concept 2, Supporting Concept 3

This image outlines how your brain will organize information when you become proficient with this skill. Your mind is literally creating a map for your thoughts to follow. Using the language of the *Five Buckets of Leadership: Speaking in the Moment*, the bubble with the original big idea (Step Two) would be the *identified bucket*, the bubbles with the specific details (Step Three)

[18] "Concept Maps," The Learning Center, University of North Carolina at Chapel Hill, https://learningcenter.unc.edu/tips-and-tools/using-concept-maps/

51

would be the *bucket carries/beliefs,* and the bubbles with the supporting concepts (Step Four) would be your *specific ideas based on your vision.*

The *Five Buckets of Leadership: Speaking in the Moment* visual would look as follows:

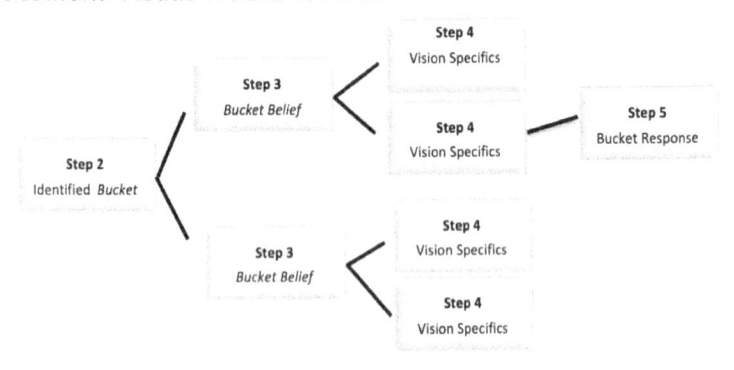

```
                          Step 4
                          Vision Specifics
          Step 3
          Bucket Belief                          Step 5
                          Step 4                 Bucket Response
                          Vision Specifics
Step 2
Identified Bucket
                          Step 4
          Step 3          Vision Specifics
          Bucket Belief
                          Step 4
                          Vision Specifics
```

Focusing your mind to think this way is central to this technique.

Step 5: *Smile and answer the question*

Smiling? The last step in the process is smiling? As simplistic as it sounds, I am sure you will be interested in knowing the effects smiling has in the brain. In 2019, SCL Health reported the following:

> *"When you smile, your brain releases tiny molecules called neuropeptides to help fight off stress. Then other neurotransmitters like dopamine, serotonin and endorphins come into play too. The endorphins act as a mild pain reliever, whereas the serotonin is an antidepressant. One study even suggests that smiling can help us recover faster from stress and reduce our heart rate. In fact, it might even be worth your while to fake a smile and see where it gets you. There's been some evidence*

that forcing a smile can still bring you a boost in your mood and happiness level." [19]

Who knew smiling was more than a way of expressing pleasure? It releases what some people call "happy hormones" that aid in combating stress. Depending on the level of intensity of what you are facing, you will need all of the help you can get to stop stress from rewiring your thoughts, but most importantly, from shrinking your brain.

Did you know there are 19 different types of smiles? Neither did I, until I started researching the topic. There is the embarrassed smile, the qualifier smile, the fear smile, and the Duchenne smile (also known as the genuine smile), just to name a few. According to Gorvett, six smiles out of the 19, are associated with happiness.[20]

Although SCL Health reported you should force a smile, Joseph Stromberg in the Smithsonian Magazine stated, "If you can manage a genuine, Duchenne smile—what people often refer to as 'smiling with your eyes,' not just your mouth—that's even better...[because it] involves the use of eye muscles, as well as those around the mouth."[21]

Simply put, your entire face is smiling. Please know the real-time moment may be too stress-induced, resulting in your inability to put on a Duchenne smile. Therefore, fake it until you make it. Force yourself to put on a happy

---

19 "The Real Health Benefits of Smiling and Laughing." SCL Health, 2019, www.scl-health.org/blog/2019/06/the-real-health-benefits-of-smiling-and-laughing.
20 Gorvett, Zaria. "Why All Smiles Are Not the Same." BBC.Com, 10 Apr. 2016, www.bbc.com/future/article/20170407-why-all-smiles-are-not-the-same.
21 Stromberg, Joseph. "Simply Smiling Can Reduce Stress." Smithsonianmag.Com, 31 July 2012, www.smithsonianmag.com/science-nature/simply-smiling-can-actually-reduce-stress-10461286.

face. Remember, the smile—whether forced or genuine—releases "happy hormones" that will not only help you fight the stress but will also help to reroute your brain's neurotransmitters.

Now that you have a theoretical understanding behind each step of the seemingly simplistic technique, let us put it into action. When questions are asked in a particular profession, they usually range from being very general to very specific. It is important for you to be able to concretely answer both types. We will start with a general question and unpack the *Five Buckets of Leadership: Speaking in the Moment* Technique.

Imagine you are in a school board meeting, and you are asked the following question: "What is your belief about safety?" At the conclusion of the question, train your mind to immediately engage in the *Five Buckets of Leadership: Speaking in the Moment* as outlined in the charts on the following pages:

Phase 5: Bucket Response

General Question Asked: "What is your belief about safety?"	

Five Buckets of Leadership Thought Process	
1. Breathe and internally identify the bucket with which the question aligns.	Safety
2. Retrieve your bucket belief to form the basis of your response.	It is a non-negotiable and extends beyond physical to one's emotional and psychological well-being.
3. Include specifics from your vision and vision carriers based on the nature of the question.	None needed because the question is general.
4. Smile and answer the question.	"I believe safety is a non-negotiable and it encompasses more than the physical well-being of individuals. For me, it also includes the emotional and psychological well-being of all students and staff."

Specific Question Asked: "Our school has had a rise in bullying incidents causing a few students to feel levels of anxiety about coming to school. What is your plan to address this concern?"

	Five Buckets of Leadership Thought Process	
1. Breathe and internally identify the bucket with which the question aligns.	Safety	
2. Retrieve your bucket belief to form the basis of your response.	It is a non-negotiable and extends beyond physical to one's emotional and psychological well-being.	
3. Include specifics from your vision and vision carriers based on the nature of the question.	**Specifics from Vision**: Create a safe-haven for students	
	Vision Carriers:	Specifics that align with the Vision Carriers:
	1. Intensive small-group instruction	Advisory groups, peer mediation, or counseling;
	2. A plethora of critical thinking opportunities (in written and oral formats)	opportunities to analyze case studies to develop language to express our views in healthy ways and develop an intellectual understanding of consequences;
	3. Student-led discussions	Engage in structured talks to gain a deeper understanding of the impact of our choices and the impact of intended or unintended consequences.

4. Smile and answer the question.	"I believe safety is a non-negotiable and it encompasses more than the physical well-being of individuals. For me, it also includes the emotional and psychological well-being of all students and staff. Therefore, I am committed to creating a safe-haven for all members of the school community, especially students. The goal is to create a place where they feel welcomed and accepted. The type of behavior you describe has no place in this safe-haven. One way we can create this safe-haven will involve us incorporating advisory groups where students analyze similar case studies to develop language that will allow them to express their views in healthy ways. It is crucial that students develop their voice. It will also be a time for them to develop an intellectual understanding of consequences. These groups will afford students the opportunity to lead the discussions so others can learn about the impact of such choices and the intended or unintended consequences. This will be a heavy lift that will require all stakeholders, so we will facilitate sessions for the entire community to become informed and involved."

Take a breath! That was a lot. You may be thinking, "Well, of course, you were able to craft such a solid response. You are sitting down writing it." However true this may be, I assure you if you allow yourself to engage in and master this technique, you will be amazed at your ability to answer questions and respond in meaningful and impactful ways. You may not be able to stop the onslaught you feel daily, but you will be able to manage it so that it does not overwhelm you. Now, take a moment and try it for yourself.

Five Buckets of Leadership: Speaking in the Moment

Consider a general question that would be posed in your organization. Write it in the table below. Next, work through each step of the process and write your responses.

General Question Asked:

Five Buckets of Leadership Thought Process	
1. Breathe and internally identify the bucket with which the question aligns.	
2. Retrieve your bucket belief to form the basis of your response.	
3. Include specifics from your vision and vision carriers based on the nature of the question.	
4. Smile and answer the question.	

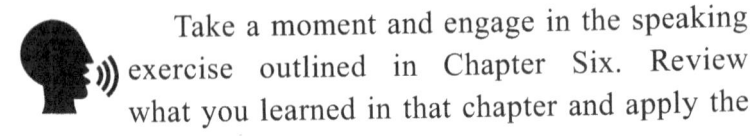

Take a moment and engage in the speaking exercise outlined in Chapter Six. Review what you learned in that chapter and apply the

Phase 5: Bucket Response

technique here with each of these steps. Now, repeat the process with a more specific question.

Specific Question Asked:

Five Buckets of Leadership Thought Process	
1. Breathe and internally identify the bucket with which the question aligns.	
2. Retrieve your bucket belief to form the basis of your response.	
3. Include specifics from your vision and vision carriers based on the nature of the question.	Specifics from Vision: <table><tr><td>Vision Carriers</td><td>Specifics that align with the Vision Carriers:</td></tr><tr><td>1.</td><td></td></tr><tr><td>2.</td><td></td></tr><tr><td>3.</td><td></td></tr></table>

Five Buckets of Leadership: Speaking in the Moment

4. Smile and answer the question.	

Stop here and practice again following the method in the previous chapter.

If you are struggling with this entire process, that is normal. We all experience difficulty when engaging in new learning. Remember, rich, deep learning requires your mind to struggle to make sense of what is presented. In the world of academia, particularly mathematics, it is called "productive struggle." The goal of productive struggle "…is to help [you] make sense of problems and persevere in solving them, no matter how difficult [you] find them to be."[22] This is the goal of the *Five Buckets of Leadership* Thought Process.

One sticking point I have found when leaders engage in this process is their knowledge base as it applies to their ability to decide on methods or techniques that align with their vision carriers. Referring back to my example for the more specific question asked, focus on my first bucket carrier—intensive small group instruction. You will notice I was able to align it with advisory groups, peer mediation, or counseling. If I were not knowledgeable of such practices, it would be difficult for me to identify specifics that aligned.

Consequently, if this information were not a part of my wheelhouse, my mind would be struggling to craft

---

[22] Franceschin, T., (2016, November, 4). How can 'productive struggle' lead to richer learning?.Edu4Me.http://edu4.me/en/how-can-productive-struggle-lead-to-richerlearning

an answer. This would cause one to be in the situation described at the start of this book. (Cue sweaty palms, racing heart, and dry mouth.) To lessen the aforementioned anxiety-producing effects, one must grow their core knowledge base. For me, this is accomplished by constantly reading, searching the internet, watching videos, or even talking with seasoned and novice colleagues. I also talk with, read after, and learn from leaders who are not in the field of education. Without this seemingly wide base of information to draw from, my skill set would be limited; thus, impacting my response time and ability to craft a solid answer. If you find yourself struggling to identify specifics that align with your vision carriers, consider reading more, watching more training videos, or even surrounding yourself with leaders who are experiencing the type of success you desire. The more you know, the more polished your answers will be.

Chapter Seven Recap:

Although muscles do not technically have a memory, we can train the nerves to respond in specific ways. Creating a training process for the mind can help how you think and respond.

Science supports the five-step process by explaining what occurs in your brain while engaging in it. Each step interrupts the brain's normal way of operating by creating "intellectual muscle memory."

1. In your own words, what is "intellectual muscle memory," and why is it important in this process?

___

2. In your own words, briefly explain the science behind each step.

Step 1: *Breathe Deeply*

___

Step 2: *Identify the bucket with which the question aligns.*

___

Step 3: *Retrieve your bucket belief to form the basis of your response.*

Step 4: *Include specifics from your vision and vision carriers based on the nature of the question.*

Step 5: *Smile and answer the question*

Troubleshooting the Process

Well, that is it! That is the *Five Buckets of Leadership: Speaking in the Moment* in a nutshell. I hope that you found it valuable. As I stated, it might seem simple and basic. But I am confident if you practice the method as described and follow the steps in Chapter Seven, you will see a dramatic improvement in your ability to respond in stress-induced environments.

Once the skill is mastered, you will not have to consciously think about each step. It will become intellectual muscle memory. You will find your brain has created a new default setting in such high-pressured moments. In the same way that an accomplished gymnast no longer has to think about how to perform a backflip, you can train your mind to have a sound response without much thought as you solidify the technique.

If, for some reason, you are not experiencing success as I have described, reflect on the phase with which you seem to be struggling. Once identified, go through the following trouble-shooting steps to help you strengthen that area.

Phase 1- The "Main" Bucket.

If you find it difficult to imagine what you want, or perhaps you have never really thought about it, consider identifying people you admire or find yourself wanting "to pattern yourself after." If you can, engage him or her in a conversation to garner nuggets about what draws you. Ask yourself, "What is it about that individual that piques my interests? Are there certain aspects of that person's life or their accomplishments I want to emulate?"

Perhaps it is a combination of people that seem to influence your wants, wishes, and desires. If there is no person you connect with, I offer you the opportunity to sit and write about why you do the things you do. Why do you keep getting up every morning to do what you do? Why do you believe you are here? Once you can identify your "why," the rest will come. For me, I pray and allow God to give me divine direction. I have found it to be the best path to follow.

Phase 2- Bucket Carriers

Many people rarely experience difficulty with this phase. The reason is that many people know what they want to do. If asked, you can probably rattle off a list of "things" you want to do. The rub or difficulty comes when those "things" do not align with your why. (Refer to Chapter Three to review the meaning of your "why.") The lack of alignment is most likely a result of your list being a buffet of unrelated things, or it is simply not specific enough.

Therefore, take a moment to review what you want to do. Ask yourself, "Is it simply a list? Is it too generic?" If you answered yes to those inquiries, take a moment to revise or rewrite your list. If you choose to approach this phase from the standpoint of *"What is my why?"* ask yourself, *"Why do I continue to get up in the morning to do what I do?"* Your answer may be based on your love for the work, need to provide, or feeling that this is the way life decided your fate. Whatever your reason, once you know the answer, the "what" becomes clearer and more impactful; hence, you should now be able to develop a more definitive list. If you are struggling to find an answer or are unhappy with this new-found realization, perhaps you may need to consider some life changes or seek some professional advice.

Phase 3 - Bucket Identification

How many people do you know who are really familiar with and understand the vision and mission of the company that employs them? Let alone, do they know the company's core values? Most people receive the employees' handbook and never read it. This happens to all of us in some form or another. A prime example is when your cell phone company asks you to read a long document about their policies. Raise your hand if you quickly scroll to the bottom to click the "accept and continue" button. Please know my hand is up too.

Notwithstanding this fact, at some point, I challenge you to read your company's document as well as get to know and understand the central beliefs of your organization. Understanding them will potentially give you the needed insight to identify what are the recurring themes your company addresses. If, after re-engaging in this manner, you still feel stuck, I encourage you to find other leaders in your field and ask them to highlight the top five recurring topics in your specific business arena. Use that as your starting place to move out of this phase.

Phase 4 – Bucket Belief

Lack of success with this phase has little to do with your company but everything to do with how well you know yourself. In Hamlet, Shakespeare pens, "To thine own self be true...."[23] It seems this well-known excerpt holds weight today because the modern-day version – *Live your truth!* – has been quoted, hashtagged, and shouted from the mountain tops on numerous occasions by celebrities and laymen alike. The subtext of both phrases implies authenticity in how you live. Before moving forward in this or the final phase step, take a personal assessment to analyze if your outward expression matches your inward character. If not, well, now is a great time to meditate, reflect, and make changes so that there is coherence. Without it, there is always that room of possibility for being perceived as disingenuous.

Phase 5 – Bucket Response

Struggle with this phrase can be summed up in this

---
23 (Hamlet, Act-1, Scene-III, 78–82)

Troubleshooting the Process

simple expression, "Practice makes perfect." This quote implies if you practice, then you will have a perfect outcome. I beg to differ because there is a fallacy associated with this phrase. What it fails to mention is the type of practice in which you engage.

For all of my football enthusiasts, we know finger placement is key to throwing a football with speed and accuracy. What if you practiced throwing a football for hours a day without implementing this one essential skill? You would be able to throw the ball but would fail to obtain the all-important spiral. You would have invested time in practicing the wrong way. You may even become "perfect" in the wrong way. With that understanding, the phrase "Perfect practice makes perfect" is more apropos. So, how does one engage in perfect practice with a skill that is learned in a book?

First, ask yourself, have you followed the steps exactly as they were written? If not, then go back and precisely follow them. If you have been true to the steps, try soliciting the assistance of one of your contemporaries to provide critical feedback in real-time and/or of one of your recorded practice sessions. Your colleague should be someone you trust, respect, and will provide action-based feedback. This type of response goes beyond saying, "That was nice!" or "You need more work!" Action-based feedback incorporates ideas and steps that can be immediately implemented so you can get and be better at what you desire to accomplish.

As with any new learning, it will take some time to master. This technique is not different and will not be mastered overnight; however, the more you intentionally

69

practice it, the technique will become a seamless process. It is my desire to strengthen leaders in every arena with becoming skilled and polished "Speakers in the Moment."

I would love to hear about the successes you have had. Please email your testimonials to GiantStep6LLC.com.

ABOUT THE AUTHOR

DR. ANISSA REILLY has been in education for over 30 years; sixteen of which as an elementary school principal in a large urban school district. She received her undergraduate degree from Morgan State University in Baltimore, Maryland, her master's degree from Bank Street College of Education, and her doctorate from The Sage Colleges of Albany. She is the president and owner of Giant Step 6 LLC. Her primary goal and passion as the senior consultant is to develop national and global leaders so they can effectively lead their perspective organization. She is the loving wife of Gordon Reilly Jr. and the mother of four amazing young adults. She has received proclamations from New York State Senator Jose Serrano and New York City Council Woman Vanessa Gibson for her assistance with improving the lives of the people in her community. "5 Buckets of Leadership: Speaking in the Moment" is the first book in her leadership series. The date for the release of her children's book series about an African-American female educational superhero named, Dr. Action, is soon to be scheduled.

FOR MORE INFORMATION

website: www.giantstep6llc.com
email address: giantstep6llc@gmail.com

Made in the USA
Middletown, DE
26 November 2019

CONGRATULATIONS YOU MADE IT THROUGH THE 30 DAYS.

PLEASE SHARE YOUR JOURNEY WITH US.

enneagramjournal.co

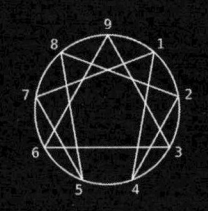

PRAYERS ANSWERED

2 Thessalonians 3:3

But the Lord is faithful. He will establish you and guard you against the evil one.

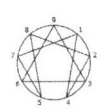

Psalm 118:14

The Lord is my strength and my song; he has become my salvation.

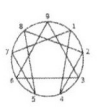

2 Timothy 4:17

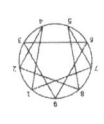

But the Lord stood by me and strengthened me, so that through me the message might be fully proclaimed and all the Gentiles might hear it. So I was rescued from the lion's mouth.

Psalm 23:4

Even though I walk through the valley of the shadow of death, I will fear no evil, for you are with me; your rod and your staff, they comfort me.

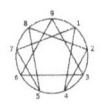

Matthew 6:33

But seek first the kingdom of God and his righteousness, and all these things will be added to you.

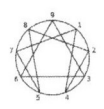

1 Peter 4:11

Whoever speaks, as one who speaks oracles of God; whoever serves, as one who serves by the strength that God supplies—in order that in everything God may be glorified through Jesus Christ. To him belong glory & dominion forever and ever. Amen.

John 16:33

I have said these things to you, that in me you may have peace. In the world you will have tribulation. But take heart; I have overcome the world.

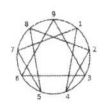

Psalm 29:11

May the Lord give strength to his people! May the Lord bless his people with peace!

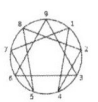

Habakkuk 3:19

God, the Lord, is my strength; he makes my feet like the deer's; he makes me tread on my high places. To the choirmaster: with stringed instruments.

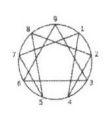

Psalm 46:1

To the choirmaster. Of the Sons of Korah. According to Alamoth. A Song.

God is our refuge and strength, a very present help in trouble.

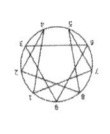

Nehemiah 8:10

Then he said to them, "Go your way. Eat the fat and drink sweet wine and send portions to anyone who has nothing ready, for this day is holy to our Lord. And do not be grieved, for the joy of the Lord is your strength."

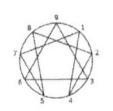

Mark 12:30

And you shall love the Lord your God with all your heart and with all your soul and with all your mind and with all your strength.

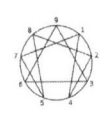

2 Corinthians 12:9

But he said to me, "My grace is sufficient for you, for my power is made perfect in weakness." Therefore I will boast all the more gladly of my weaknesses, so that the power of Christ may rest upon me.

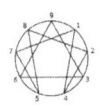

Psalm 73:26

My flesh and my heart may fail, but God is the strength of my heart and my portion forever.

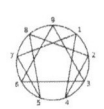

Psalm 31:24

Be strong, and let your heart take courage, all you who wait for the Lord!

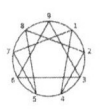

Psalm 27:1

Of David. The Lord is my light and my salvation; whom shall I fear? The Lord is the stronghold of my life; of whom shall I be afraid?

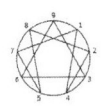

Isaiah 40:29

He gives power to the faint, and to him who has no might he increases strength.

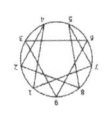

Matthew 11:28

Come to me, all who labor and are heavy laden, and I will give you rest.

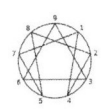

Isaiah 12:2

Behold, God is my salvation; I will trust, and will not be afraid; for the Lord God is my strength and my song, and he has become my salvation.

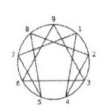

2 Timothy 1:7

For God gave us a spirit not of fear but of power and love and self-control.

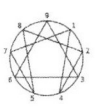

Joshua 1:9

Have I not commanded you? Be strong & courageous. Do not be frightened, and do not be dismayed, for the Lord your God is with you wherever you go.

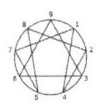

2 Corinthians 12:9-10

But he said to me, "My grace is sufficient for you, for my power is made perfect in weakness." Therefore I will boast all the more gladly of my weaknesses, so that the power of Christ may rest upon me. For the sake of Christ, then, I am content with weaknesses, insults, hardships, persecutions, and calamities. For when I am weak, then I am strong.

Deuteronomy 20:4

For the Lord your God is he who goes with you to fight for you against your enemies, to give you the victory.

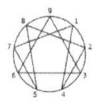

Ephesians 6:10

Finally, be strong in the Lord and in the strength of his might.

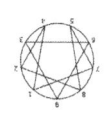

Exodus 15:2

The Lord is my strength and my song, and he has become my salvation; this is my God, and I will praise him, my father's God, and I will exalt him.

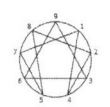

1 Corinthians 10:13

No temptation has overtaken you that is not common to man. God is faithful, & He will not let you be tempted beyond your ability, but with the temptation he will also provide the way of escape, that you may be able to endure it.

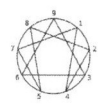

Isaiah 40:31

But they who wait for the Lord shall renew their strength; they shall mount up with wings like eagles; they shall run and not be weary; they shall walk and not faint.

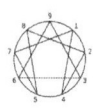

Deuteronomy 31:6

Be strong and courageous. Do not fear or be in dread of them, for it is the Lord your God who goes with you. He will not leave you or forsake you.

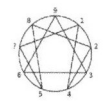

Isaiah 41:10

Fear not, for I am with you; be not dismayed, for I am your God; I will strengthen you, I will help you, I will uphold you with my righteous right hand.

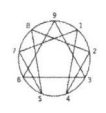

Philippians 4:13

I can do all things through him who strengthens me.

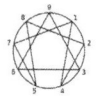

In the journaling pages we have pulled a verse and study questions for you to meditate on each morning. Each verse has been curated to envoke and stir reflection to your specific Ennaegram type.

Read and Respond on the lines, Enjoy the Journey >>

Now that you have learned the Enneagram types.

Let us introduce you to your customized prayer journal >>

Nines essentially feel a need for peace and harmony. They tend to avoid conflict at all costs, whether it be internal or interpersonal. As the potential for conflict in life is virtually ubiquitous, the Nine's desire to avoid it generally results in some degree of withdrawal from life, and many Nines are, in fact, introverted. Other Nines lead more active, social lives, but nevertheless remain to some to degree "checked out," or not fully involved, as if to insulate themselves from threats to their peace of mind.

Type 9

Keeping peace and harmony.

Eights are essentially unwilling to be controlled, either by others or by their circumstances; they fully intend to be masters of their fate. Eights are strong willed, decisive, practical, tough minded and energetic.

They also tend to be domineering; their unwillingness to be controlled by others frequently manifests in the need to control others instead.

Type 8

Taking charge, because they don't want to be controlled.

Sevens are essentially concerned that their lives be an exciting adventure. They are future oriented, restless people who are generally convinced that something better is just around the corner. They are quick thinkers who have a great deal of energy and who make lots of plans. They tend to be extroverted, multi-talented, creative and open minded.

Type 7

Pleasure seekers and planners, in search of distraction.

Sixes essentially feel insecure, as though there is nothing quite steady enough to hold onto. At the core of the type Six personality is a kind of fear or anxiety. Sixes don't trust easily; they are often ambivalent about others, until the person has absolutely proven herself, at which point they are likely to respond with steadfast loyalty.

Type 6

Conflicted between trust and distrust.

Fives essentially fear that they don't have enough inner strength to face life, so they tend to withdraw, to retreat into the safety and security of the mind where they can mentally prepare for their emergence into the world. Fives feel comfortable and at home in the realm of thought. They are generally intelligent, well read and thoughtful and they frequently become experts in the areas that capture their interest.

Type 5

Thinkers who tend to withdraw and observe.

Fours build their identities around their perception of themselves as being somehow different or unique; they are thus self-consciously individualistic. They tend to see their difference from others as being both a gift and a curse - a gift, because it sets them apart from those they perceive as being somehow "common," and a curse, as it so often seems to separate them from the simpler forms of happiness that others so readily seem to enjoy.

Type 4

Identity seekers, who feel unique and different.

Threes need to be validated in order to feel worthy; they pursue success and want to be admired. They are frequently hard working, competetive and are highly focused in the pursuit of their goals, whether their goal is to be the most successful salesman in the company or the "sexiest" woman in their social circle.

Type 3

Focused on the presentation of success, to attain validation.

Twos essentially feel that they are worthy insofar as they are helpful to others. Love is their highest ideal. Selflessness is their duty.

Giving to others is their reason for being.

Involved, socially aware, usually extroverted, Twos are the type of people who remember everyone's birthday and who go the extra mile to help out a co-worker, spouse or friend in need.

Type 2

Helpers who need to be needed.

Ones are essentially looking to make things better, as they think nothing is ever quite good enough. This makes them perfectionists who want to reform and improve, who desire to make order out of the omnipresent chaos.

Type 1

Perfectionists, responsible, fixated on improvement

WINGS

Usually one has characteristics of one of the types that lie adjacent to one's own that are more prominent. This is called the wing. So someone who is a type 5, might have a 4 wing or a 6 wing. This may be abbreviated to "5w4" and "5w6". If one doesn't have a dominant wing, it is said that the wings are balanced

People of a particular type have several characteristics in common, but they can be quite different nevertheless.

>>

Which are you? >>

1. The Reformer
2. The Helper
3. The Achiever
4. The Individualist
5. The Investigator
6. The Loyalist
7. The Enthusiast
8. The Challenger
9. The Peacemaker

The Enneagram is a personality typing system that consists of nine different types. Everyone is considered to be one single type, although one can have traits belonging to other ones.

While it's uncertain whether this type is genetically determined, many believe it is already in place at birth.

The nine types (or "enneatypes", "ennea" means "nine") are universally identified by the numbers 1 to 9.

These numbers have a standard way of being placed around the Enneagram symbol. Enneagram authors have attached their own individual names to these numbers they are as follows:

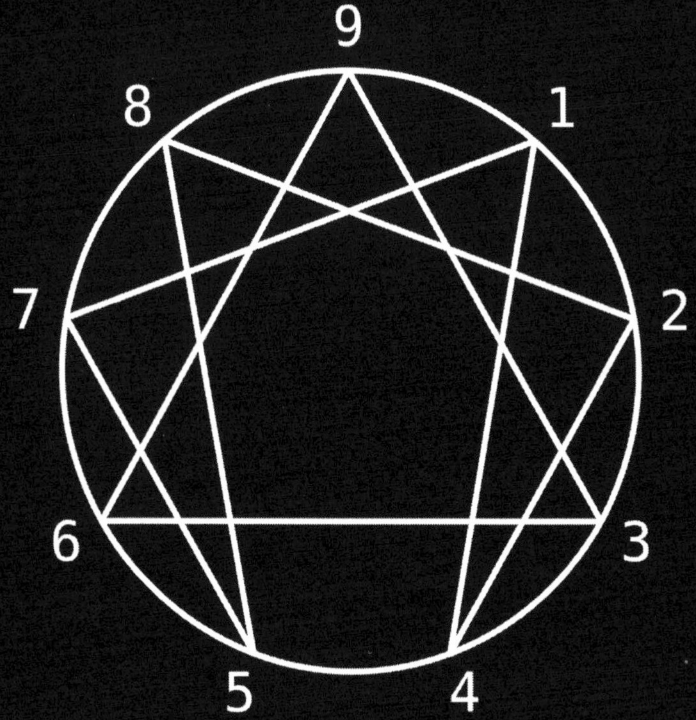
9
8
1
7
2
6
3
5
4

WHAT IS THE ENNEAGRAM?

Lets get Personal.

Who does this journal belong to?
_____

What does your relationship with Jesus look like?
_____

How often do you pray?
_____

City & State you live in?
_____

Do you currently attend a church? If so, what do you love about it?
_____

Group of friends that you will journal with to keep accountable to:
_____

THE ENNEAGRAM PRAYER JOURNAL

Created to remind you of God's Goodness in every season.

Published by Journal Hub
Los Angeles, California

Copyright © My Prayer Journal 2019

Scripture quotations marked (NIV) are taken from the THE HOLY BIBLE, NEW INTERNATIONAL VERSION®, NIV® Copyright © 1973, 1978, 1984, 2011 by Biblica, Inc.™ Used by permission. All rights reserved worldwide.

If you are interested in bulk orders for your church or organization, message us at enneagramjournal.co/contact

IF FOUND PLEASE KINDLY RETURN TO:

Y0-DEY-755

NAME:

_____

CELL:

_____